Cornwall
From the Air

First published in Great Britain in 2010 by
The Derby Books Publishing Company Limited
3 The Parker Centre,
Derby, DE21 4SZ.

A catalogue record for this book is available from the
British Library.

ISBN 978-1-85983-800-6

Printed and bound by Progress Press, Malta.

John Such

Cornwall

From the Air

DB PUBLISHING

ACKNOWLEDGEMENTS

I would like to thank the following people: Richard Elwell at Elburydesign.com for all my corporate design and art direction, but mostly for his valued friendship; Cornwall Flying Club, Captain Matt and all of the pilots I have flown with including Keith, Duncan and Kevin at Castle Air; DB Publishing for recognising my talent and signing me for this book and others in the future; Keith Appleby, my photography tutor over 25 years ago; and I would like to thank Hel, Bex & Ems, the three ladies in my life! Finally, I want to thank all of my friends, family and clients who have supported me over the years.

John Such, 2010

INTRODUCTION

Cornwall is a unique place, and flying over the county at anything from 200-1,500ft gives me a fantastic viewpoint not shared by many.

I fly in helicopters and light aircraft, with most of my work being commissioned by magazines, designers, corporate companies, property developers, holiday companies and advertising agencies. Fortunately, all of the pilots I fly with have a great understanding of the kind of shots I am looking for, although it is essential that I convey to the pilot where I want the aircraft positioned so I am able to get the very best shot.

A lot of my images are shot on medium format transparency film and then scanned to digital format as a high-res jpeg. Film gives you lovely colour saturation; however, I am also shooting digitally on my new 22 million pixel camera and getting great results.

From mid-May to September the days are long, trees and fields are vibrant green and the seas surrounding Cornwall are a turquoise that would rival the Caribbean; however, even in autumn and winter we can be blessed with crisp clear sunny days that can still make for great pictures.

All of my work is weather dependent so organising aircraft and pilots can be tricky, but when everything comes together I still find it extremely rewarding capturing Cornwall at its very best. In this book I have selected a varied mix of images showing beautiful coastline, hidden coves and ancient sites, all of which make Cornwall the great county that it is.

I hope these images give you all as much pleasure as I have had in taking them!

Padstow and the Camel Estuary.

Padstow harbour, with Trevose Head
visible in the background.

The coastline near Bude.

The Eden Project, which is situated near St Austell.

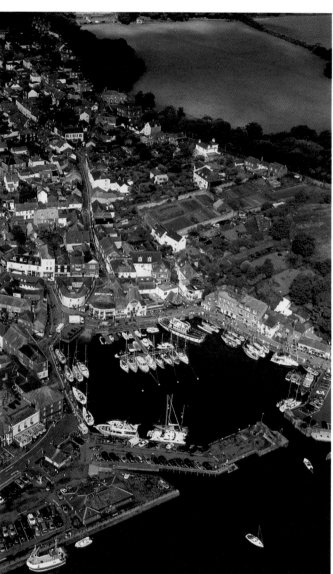

Padstow harbour on a high tide.

Polhawn Fort, near Rame Head.

Looking across Porthcothan
to Trevose Head.

Port Isaac is a small fishing port, where the television series *Doc Martin* is filmed.

13

Cliff-top houses perch above the sea in Porthcothan.

Two views of Prideaux House near Padstow.

Treyarnon Bay.

The harbour at Padstow.

The view out from
Treyarnon to Trevose Head.

Polmanter Holiday Park, which can be found near St Ives.

Boats moored in the bay at Rock.

Trevelgue and
Smugglers Haven
caravan parks near
Newquay.

23

A view of St Merryn.

Constantine Bay.

A park and ride car park outside Truro.

Trevone.

The coastline from
Daymer Bay to
Polzeath.

Bocaddon Farm produces goods such as cheese and veal.

Carlyon Bay, which features a caravan park and a golf club.

A shot of Trevone, showing the blow hole in the background.

Cliff-top homes in Polzeath.

In the middle of summer
Polzeath is a popular
surfing beach.

33

Padstow and the
Camel Estuary.

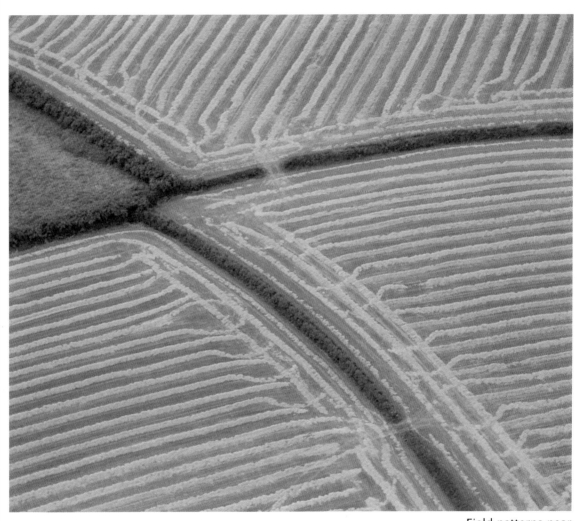

Field patterns near
Trevose Head.

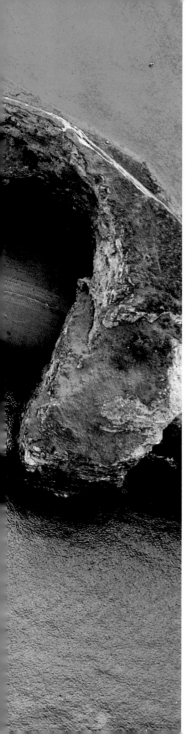

Bassetts Cove near
Portreath.

Bedruthan Steps,
near Newquay.

Bedruthan Steps on a choppy day.

Another view of
Bedruthan Steps.

The grand
Boconnoc Estate
is situated near
Lostwithiel.

The Blackpool china clay pit, near St Austell.

A view across Bodmin.

A view across to St Mawes on the south coast.

Caerhays Castle and grounds.

Speed boats on the
Camel Estuary.

The village of Carnkie near Redruth, with Carn Brea monument on the hill in the background.

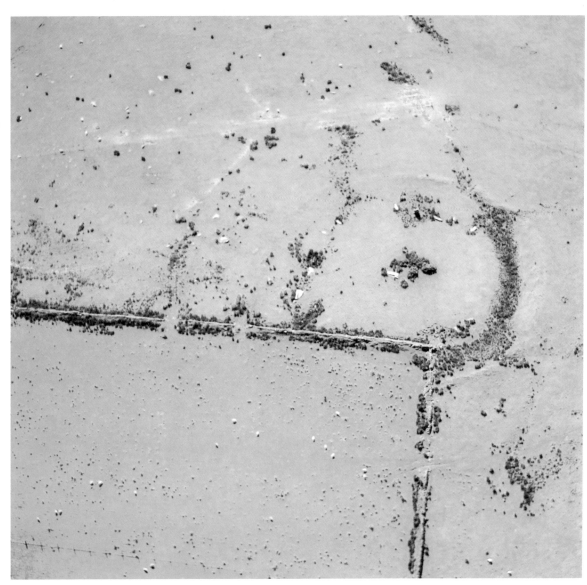

An ancient stone circle on Bodmin Moor.

A view of Constantine Bay and Trevose Golf Club.

A boat approaches the harbour in Coverack.

The beach at Crantock.

Crantock, near Newquay.

A cruise liner moored up in Fowey.

Cubert, near Holywell Bay.

Looking out to Holywell Bay from Cubert.

St Enodoc Church and
Daymer Bay.

Cattle grazing in vibrant
green fields.

A boat heads in to
Penzance.

Gorran Haven, near Mevagissey.

Hannafore, near Looe.

Calm seas in Holywell Bay.

The crystal clear sea off
Holywell Bay.

The cliffs of Housel Bay,
near the Lizard.

The quaint villages of
Kingsand and Cawsand,
which can be found on the
south coast.

Kynance Cove.

A view of Land's End.

Looking along the cliffs to Land's End.

The Lizard.

The Lizard lighthouse and coastline.

The coastline between
Mullion Cove and the Lizard.

Looe at high tide in
mid-summer.

The coastline near Land's End.

The lookout tower near Mousehole on the south coast.

St Michael's Mount, which can be found off the coast near Penzance.

The beach at Mawgan Porth, near Newquay.

The fishing port of
Mevagissey.

Millbrook.

Minack Theatre has been built
into the cliffs at Porthcurno.

Mother Ivey's Bay near Trevose Head.

Mullion Cove.

77

Nare Head is located
on the south coast
near Veryan.

Looking out to Nare Head.

Newlyn harbour on a hazy summer day.

A view of Polzeath.

A secluded cove near Polruan.

A view of Padstow harbour.

High tide in Newquay.

The dunes of
Penhale Sands.

Pentire Head, near Newquay.

A view of Penzance on a hazy day.

Perranporth.

Another view of Perranporth.

Looking across from
Picklecombe Fort to Drake's
Island and Plymouth.

Picklecombe Fort was built
in the mid–19th century.

The picturesque village of Polperro.

A view of the high cliffs at Mevagissey.

Polzeath.

Porth Island, which is located near Newquay.

Clear, tranquil sea near Portscatho.

Porthcothan.

Porthcurnick Beach.

A turquoise lagoon
near Porthcurno.

Another view of
Porth Island.

Porthleven, which is
located near Helston.

A view of Porthtowan.

Porthminster, near St Ives.

The village of Portloe nestles behind its cliffs.

A yacht moored up in the
bay at Portmellon.

Portreath.

Portscatho.

Another view of Portscatho.

Cottages tucked away
in Prussia Cove.

Restronguet Point.

Pentire and the River Gannel near Newquay.

The coastline near Trevose Head.

111

Looking out to sea above
the village of Rock.

A view of the beach at Seaton.

A view of St Anthony Head.

St Ives.

Looking out over St Just in Roseland.

St Tudy.

Turquoise waters off St Ives.

Symbol in the fields of
Bodmin Moor.

Talland Bay.

Treago Farm Caravan Park
near Holywell Bay.

Trebah Gardens on
Helford Passage.

Trebetherick and
Daymer Bay.

123

Trevone.

Another view of Trevone.

Trewavas Mine.

Truro is the only city within the county of Cornwall.

Wadebridge.

127

Restronguet Point, Feock.

LIGHTNING
STRIKES

Previous page: F.2 of 19 Squadron, which began conversion from the Hunter F.6 to the Lightning F.2 at Leconfield late in 1962. The first of a dozen F.2s were received on 17 December 1962. F.2s were configured with four 30 mm Aden cannon, the lower guns displacing the two Firestreaks, while the F.2As were F.2s rebuilt to incorporate some F.6 features such as kinked and cambered wing, square-cut fin of greater area, and an enlarged ventral fuel tank, two Aden cannon in the upper nose, and two AAMs (Air to Air Missiles). 19 Squadron moved to Gütersloh, eighty miles from the East German border, on 23 September 1965. Here they began patrolling the air identification zone. The role increasingly saw the F.2s and F.2As of 19 (and 92 Squadron, which moved from Leconfield to Gelsenkirchen at the end of December 1965, and whose re-equipment with the F.2A was concluded in 1969) used in low-level interception. (*Brian Allchin*)

Opposite: Lightnings in their element. The 1A's two Rolls-Royce Avons with reheat produced 11,250 lbs of thrust 'dry' and around 14,000 lbs 'wet'. Fuel capacity with the 250 gallon ventral tank installed was 1,020 gallons (with 40 gallons unusable). All fuel shown on the two fuel gauges was 'usable'. Weight was around fourteen tons with full fuel load. Once the ventral tank was empty the power-to-weight ratio was better than 1 lb of thrust to 1 lb of weight. Fuel consumption at idle (31%) was 156 gallons/hour per engine. At 100% (maximum power) with reheat, it was 3,119 gallons/hour per engine. Sortie time was normally around 45–50 minutes. With reheat on, practice interceptions could be maintained for 20–25 minutes. When accelerating from a standing start, most modern motorcycles would reach 60 mph before the Lightning, but after 60 mph, the Lightning would be at 5,000 feet before the motorcycle reached maximum speed! (*Dick Bell*)

LIGHTNING STRIKES

English Electric's Supersonic Fighter in Action

MARTIN W. BOWMAN

Airlife
England

Acknowledgements

Tony Aldridge; Brian Allchin; Dick Bell; John Bryant; Denis G. Calvert; Edwin Carter; Cobham PLC; Dick Doleman; Malcolm English; Jan Govaerts; David Grimer; John Hale; Peter Hayward; Ken Hazell; Grp Capt. Mike Hobson CBE; Grp Capt. W.B.G. Hopkins; Mick Jennings; Jimmy Jewell; Graham Mitchell; Pete Nash; Tony Paxton; Ritchie Pymar; Mike Rigg; Grp Capt. Dave Roome OBE MRAeS RAF; Sqn Ldr Clive Rowley; Adrian Savage; Grp Capt. Dave Seward AFC; Peter Symes; Thunder City Entertainments; Hugh Trevor; Graham Vernon; Grp Capt. P.T.G. Webb OBE DL.

First published in the UK in 2001
by Airlife Publishing Ltd

British Library Cataloguing-in-Publication Data
A catalogue record for this book
is available from the British Library

ISBN 1 84037 236 2

Printed in Singapore by Kyodo Printing Co. (S'pore) Pte Ltd.

Airlife Publishing Ltd
101 Longden Road, Shrewsbury, SY3 9EB, England
E-mail: airlife@airlifebooks.com
Website: www.airlifebooks.com

Introduction

On 11 August 1954, on only its third flight, P.1A WG760, flown by Wg Cdr Roland P. 'Bee' Beamont, broke the sound barrier to become Britain's first truly supersonic jet, capable of exceeding Mach 1 in level flight. Lightnings have captured the imagination of boys of all ages ever since. After more than a quarter of a century as one of the RAF's air defence fighters, the English Electric Lightning ceased to be a front-line interceptor on 30 April 1988. The first Lightnings were delivered to the Central Fighter Establishment at RAF Coltishall, Norfolk, in December 1959 and the first squadron, 74, formed at the same station, in July 1960. Nine front-line squadrons operated the Lightning – 74, 56, 'Treble-One', 19, 92, 23, 5, 11, and 29. The Lightning is perhaps best remembered for its amazing take-off performance, witnessed at airfields around the world, from East Anglia and Lincolnshire, to Germany, Cyprus, and Malta and as far afield as the Far East. Its inordinately high loss rate is also etched in the memory of many. Some 334 Lightnings, including prototypes (of which five were lost), were built. Of the 253 production Lightnings operated by the RAF, 1959–1988, sixty-three were lost, resulting in forty-six pilot ejections and the death of seventeen pilots. Twenty-one of these Lightning losses are attributable to pilot error, nineteen to mechanical malfunctions, and twenty-four to fire. Grp Capt. David Seward, OC, 56 'Firebirds' Squadron, best sums up this incomparable jet fighter: *'The aeroplane was superb to fly, a bitch to maintain and always short of fuel. In hindsight, we probably wouldn't have wanted it any other way.'*

Martin W. Bowman
Norwich

Below: Lightning Sixteen. (*Dick Bell*)

T.5 XS452/ZU-BBD, one of four Lightnings owned and operated by Thunder City Entertainments in South Africa. (*Max Dereta*)

Tiger, Tiger. Line-up of 74 'Tiger' Squadron F.1s at Coltishall. Squadron Leader (later AVM) John F.G. Howe, a South African by birth, who had flown SAAF F-86 Sabres in the Korean War, had (after a short spell of instructing) taken command of the *Tigers,* the first operational squadron in Fighter Command to be equipped with the Lightning, in February 1960. XM165 was the first F.1 taken on charge at Coltishall, on 29 June 1960 and in September John Howe led formation flypasts of four aircraft at the Farnborough Air Show. A nine-ship formation was flown at Farnborough 1961, when the first public demonstration of nine Lightnings rolling in tight formation occurred. In 1962 the *Tigers* became the official Fighter Command aerobatic team. Pilot of the nearest F.1 is Flt Lt Tim J. Nelson, while the name of Chief Tech. Rye appears beneath his name on the nose. F.1 XM135 (behind) is now on permanent display at the Imperial War Museum (IWM), Duxford. (*BAe*)

56 Squadron converted to the Lightning F.1 at Wattisham, Suffolk, in December 1960. It was the first squadron to receive the F.1A, the full complement being received by March 1961. The F.1A was fitted with a port-mounted probe for in-flight refuelling and it fell to 56 Squadron to pioneer this technique in the Lightning squadrons. Sqn Ldr (later Grp Capt.) Dave Seward and his pilots began perfecting the art of air-to-air refuelling in 1962, training first on USAF F-100Ds with Boeing KC-97s as tankers, before air-refuelling in earnest in 1962 with RAF Vickers Valiant tankers. F.1A XM179/J, flown by Flt Lt Dick Cloke, here tanking from XD816. (*Via Dave Seward*)

Above: In 1963, 56 Squadron – the *Firebirds* – here taking off from Wattisham in June, became the second of the official Fighter Command Lightning aerobatic display teams. The team's name was derived from the squadron's *Phoenix rising from the ashes* emblem. (*Brian Allchin*)

Right: Pilots of 56 Squadron, dressed in khaki, puttees and stiff white collars, strike up a pose for a pseudo '1932' group photograph. **Back row L–R**: Flt Lt Mike Cooke; Flt Lt Bob Offord; Flt Lt Tim Mermagen (wearing Albert Ball VC's uniform) on horse (which started to chew John Curry's cap); Flt Lt Henry Plozeck; Flt Lt Cooper; Flt Lt 'Mac' McEwen (the solo man, later the English Electric liaison pilot); Flt Lt Bob Manning. **Middle**: Flt Lt Terry Thompson RCAF; Flt Lt Jerry Cohu (B Flt CO); Sqn Ldr Dave Seward, OC; Flt Lt John Curry; Flt Lt Mo Moore. **Front Row**: Flg Off. Dave Adam; Flt Lt 'Jimmy' Jewell; Flt Lt Ernie Jones. The photo was converted to sepia by dipping it in tea, and it was then hung on the mess wall! (*Jimmy Jewell*)

111 Squadron, known universally as 'Treble-One' (and less kindly throughout the rest of the RAF, as the *Tremblers)*, began equipping on the Lightning F.1A at Wattisham, in March 1963. Here, Flt Lt 'Bugs' Bendell, 111 Squadron solo display pilot, in F.1A XM188/F taxies in at the end of his earth-shattering (literally!) June 1963 display for students of the Royal College of Defence Studies. Bugs, who was a very charismatic character, made a high-speed run, as usual straight over the ATC tower, whereupon the doors on the Ops buildings were left hanging off their hinges and the windows in local control disintegrated, showering the visitors watching on the veranda with broken glass! An Army colonel, while flicking shards of glass off his once immaculate uniform, commented: *'I must say that when the RAF puts on a show it spares no expense!'* Ordered to report to OC Ops, with HAT ON, Bugs first had to apologise to the Met Officer, whom he found ashen-faced, and on leaving his office, noticed that his raincoat was pinned to the back of his office door by a spear of glass! When Grp Capt. David Simmonds, the station commander, finished his appraisal he told 'Bugs' to report to the MoD. When Bugs asked if it was for a punishment posting, Simmonds smiled and told him, *'No, it's about an exchange posting to the USA* [Nellis AFB flying the F-105 Thunderchief]'. Meanwhile, the inquiry found that the Met conditions had changed during the display and had 'induced' marginal supersonic flight. Bugs was nonetheless fined the equivalent of the cost of a family car in those days by way of reparation for the damage! *(Peter Symes)*

Tragedy. Flt Lt Peter Symes, recently arrived at Wattisham from Cranwell, remembers: '*After 56 was given the aerobatic commitment it was fascinating to see them gradually working up into shape. When they began to display at lower level over the airfield almost everybody used to stop to watch. Eventually, we became accustomed to their routine and they just became a noise in the background. However, on 6 June 1963, in my office on the upper floor of SHQ facing the back of the hangars, I noticed an unusual WHOOMPH as the formation did its horizontal bomb-burst head-on to the hangar line. Glancing out of the window I saw an airman outside the guardroom looking to the sky above SHQ in obvious amazement and I noticed something glinting as it tumbled down into the Airmen's Married Quarters. Realising that something had gone wrong, I dashed up onto the roof in time to see a mushroom cloud of smoke starting to drift down wind – then a Lightning starting to orbit at low level. Shortly afterwards, the wife of the Disci Sergeant* came into SHQ to see her husband. She was in a very distressed state. XM179 had thundered into a field of peas only about fifty yards from the narrow road on which she had been driving towards the Station and it had seemed to be heading straight for her.' This picture shows the still-smouldering crater left by the impact of F.1A XM179/J. The pilot, Flt Lt Mike Cooke, had hit F.1A XM171/A, flown by Flt Lt Mo Moore, during the practice bomb-burst over Wattisham. Moore managed to get XM171/A down safely at Wattisham but minus both his Firestreak missiles, which were dislodged in the collision and which fell harmlessly in the RAF Married Quarters area. Mike Cooke ejected but the dynamics were outside the Mk. 4 seat's design envelope and, though Mike survived, he suffered almost total paralysis as a result of the accident. His flying career was finished at the age of only twenty-three. (*Brian Allchin*)

Above: F.1A XM176/F of the *Firebirds*. This aircraft first flew on 1 December 1960 and was issued to 56 Squadron on 16 January 1961 as 'D'. It was recoded 'F' around March 1963. It served the *Firebirds* until February 1965, being stored until it was scrapped in August 1974. (*Richard Wilson via Brian Allchin*)

Right: The *Firebirds*, Wattisham, late summer 1963. **L–R**: Flt Lt John Curry; Flt Lt Dick Cloke; Flt Lt Brian Allchin; Flt Lt Jerry Cohu; Flt Lt Terry Thompson RCAF; Sqn Ldr Dave Seward CO; Flt Lt Jimmy Jewell; Flt Lt Bob Manning; Flt Lt Henry Plozeck; Flt Lt Mo Moore; Flt Lt Ernie Jones; Flt Lt Tim Mermagen. (*Via Brian Allchin*)

Alpha Down. F.1A XM171/A, spectacularly flown by Flt Lt Brian Allchin, photographed by Richard Wilson from the *Firebirds'* T.4 flown by Flt Lt John Curry, on 2 September 1963. XM171 first flew on 20 September 1960 and was issued to the *Firebirds* on 28 February 1961 as 'R'. It was recoded 'A' early in 1963. After serving later with 226 Operational Conversion Unit (OCU) and 60 Maintenance Unit (MU), XM171 was salvaged in March 1974 and scrapped in July that year. Immediately after coming out of the loop, the T.4 had a multiple bird strike, but it landed safely. (*Richard Wilson via Brian Allchin*)

Flt Lt Brian Mason of 111 Squadron suffered a landing mishap in F.1A XM215 at Wattisham in January 1964. This Lightning first flew on 11 July 1961 and joined 'Treble-One' Squadron on 2 August that year. XM215 was later transferred to 226 OCU (Operational Conversion Unit) at Coltishall, and the Binbrook Target Facilities Flight. (*Brian Allchin*)

F.3 XP749 first flew on 11 December 1963 and was issued to the Air Fighter Development Squadron (AFDS), where it was coded 'T', on 8 April 1964. On 22 December 1965 XP749 joined 'Treble-One' Squadron at Wattisham and later went on to serve with the Lightning Training Flight (LTF), and 11 Squadron, before being used as a decoy prior to being scrapped in late 1987. (*John Hale*)

Gas Guzzler! F.1A XM173 of 56 Squadron taking on fuel from a Vickers Valiant in January 1964 in the run-up to a detachment to Cyprus that summer. When, in January 1965, 92 Squadron's turn came to fly a detachment to Cyprus, the deployment coincided with the withdrawal from service of all Valiants after dangerous metal fatigue had been discovered in their airframes in August 1964. It meant that the Lightning pilots had to 'puddle-jump' their way to Cyprus, via Germany, France, and Sardinia! (*Brian Allchin*)

Red, white, ... 56 Squadron's distinctive all-red livery and phoenix rising from the ashes. (*Via Dave Seward*)

and 'Shiny-blue'. 92 Squadron ('Shiny-Blue')'s equally attractive royal blue and cobra-entwined emblem. (*Brian Allchin*)

Above: Flt Lt Nick Galpin (centre) of 56 Squadron dons the cover from a Firestreak missile and clowns for the camera during an Air to Air Refuelling (AAR) to Cyprus in 1964. Left is Ching Fuller. Sqn Ldr 'Hank' Martin, the new 56 Squadron OC, holds Galpin's legs. (*Brian Allchin*)

Opposite: 56 Squadron personnel in Cyprus during 1964. On the steps of F.1A XM178/H, centre, is Flt Lt Brian Allchin. Top of steps is Sqn Ldr Hank Martin, next is Flt Lt Nick Galpin, then Mike Graydon and Pete Clee. (*Brian Allchin*)

Tiger tails. F.1s of 74 Squadron newly arrived at Leuchars, Scotland, in July 1964. The nearest aircraft is XM163/K, next is XM164/L, followed by XM135/B, XM136/C, then XM137/D, 'G', XM147/J, and 'F'. XM163 first flew on 23 April 1960 and was issued to AFDS before use with 74 Squadron. XM164 first flew on 13 June 1960 and joined the *Tigers* on 15 July that year. XM135 first flew on 14 November 1959 and was issued to AFDS on 25 May 1960. It was loaned to 74 Squadron at first (as 'R') and became 'B' on a permanent basis in 1964. XM135 went to 226 OCU on 25 July 1964. This Lightning was one of several at 33 MU at Lyneham in 1966 prepared as supersonic target aircraft for Fighter Command. While carrying out taxi tests on 22 July, Wg Cdr Walter 'Taffy' Holden, a forty-year-old engineering officer and the CO of 33 MU, went for an unscheduled trip in XM135, when, on the fourth taxi run, reheat was inadvertently selected and the F.1 took off! Holden, who had never flown a jet aircraft before, was not wearing a helmet and the canopy had been removed prior to the taxi tests. Despite his lack of experience, Holden remained airborne for twelve minutes and managed to land XM135 safely at the second attempt. XM135 was repaired and used by the Leuchars Target Facilities Flight (TFF) before being retired to the IWM Collection at Duxford on 20 November 1974, where it is on permanent display. XM136 first flew on 1 December 1959 and was issued to AFDS on 21 June 1960. It too was loaned to 74 Squadron (as 'S') on 7 September 1961 and, after modifications at English Electric, returned to the Squadron as 'C'. (*Group Capt. P.T.G. Webb*)

Right: Diamonds are forever. Peter Symes did exceptionally well, without the aid of a motor drive, to capture the shock diamonds emanating from Avons in reheat, during this demonstration by F.3 XP765/N of 56 Squadron at UNISON '65 (a seminar for Air Officers, senior civil servants, and some ministers) at Cranwell in September 1965. XP765, which first flew on 26 September 1964 and joined 56 on 6 September 1965, was fitted with dummy overwing tanks for UNISON 65. Late in April 1967 XP765 joined 29 Squadron and served until late in 1974, and was then struck off charge (SOC) and scrapped in April 1975. (*Peter Symes*)

Below: Royal Navy Sea Vixen refuelling F.1A XM189/E of 'Treble-One' Squadron on 28 May 1963. XM189/E first flew on 30 March 1961 and was issued to 111 Squadron on 1 May that year. In February 1965 XM189 transferred to 226 OCU at Coltishall. It was finally withdrawn from active OCU service in June 1974, and, beginning on 10 July 1974, was used as a decoy at Gütersloh. (*Cobham PLC*)

Leconfield Lightnings. 19 Squadron's F.2s ready to leave Yorkshire on 23 September 1965 for the flight to their new posting to Gütersloh in West Germany. 92 Squadron's F.2s also left Leconfield, for Gelsenkirchen, three months later to join them in RAF Germany. (*John Hale*)

T.4 and F.2s of 19 Squadron neatly lined up after arrival at Gütersloh, September 1965. Far left is T.4 XM991/T, which first flew on 4 October 1961 and was issued to the Lightning Conversion Squadron (LCS) on 13 October 1962. After service with 226 OCU it joined 19 Squadron in August 1963. XM991/T burned out in a ground fire at Gütersloh in June 1975. (*John Hale*)

John Hale risked life and limb climbing one of the floodlights on the pan at Gütersloh to take this line-up shot of 19 Squadron! (*John Hale*)

Night falls at Gütersloh in 1965. (*John Hale*)

Left: New livery. 56 Squadron, with their distinctive (but short-lived!) chequerboard tails, climbing over East Anglia in 1965. (*Brian Allchin*)

Below: 56 Squadron's F.3s taxi out at Luqa during the Malta Air Defence Exercise (ADEX) in October 1965. (*Brian Allchin*)

F.3s of 56 Squadron lined up at Luqa, Malta, in 1965. The nearest aircraft is XP746/K, which first flew on 26 March 1964 and joined the squadron on 15 April 1965. It joined 'Treble One' Squadron on 4 August 1970 and was struck off charge in April 1975. (*Graham Vernon*)

Flt Lt Tony Aldridge of 23 Squadron maintains close formation on take-off from RAF Leuchars, Scotland, with Lightning F.3 XP763/M in 1965. XP763 first flew on 11 September 1964 and was issued to 23 Squadron on 27 October 1964. It went to 60 MU in July 1966 and later flew with 56 and 29 Squadrons before being struck off charge and scrapped in March 1975. (*Tony Aldridge*)

T.4 XM997 of 226 OCU from RAF Coltishall over the North Sea in September 1965. (Note the all-black Firestreak missile). This T-bird first flew on 22 May 1962 and was originally delivered to the OCU at RAF Middleton St George on 14 January 1963. (*Jimmy Jewell*)

F.2 XN787/M of 19 Squadron from Leconfield off the Yorkshire coast in the late 1960s. XN787 first flew on 15 February 1963 and was issued to 19 Squadron on 22 March that year. On 1 July 1969 it was returned to BAC for conversion to F.2A and on 20 May 1970 it was reissued to 92 Squadron, coded 'L'. It was allocated to Laarbruch on New Year's Eve 1976 for decoy duties. (*MoD*)

Pilots of 5 Squadron and their junior engineering officer smile for the camera during a break from practice firing at the Aberporth ranges, Wales, in November 1965. **L–R**: Flt Lt Neil Davidson, Flt Lt Bill Gambold, Flt Lt Brian Allchin (pilot of F.3 XR765/M, behind), Sqn Ldr 'Bunny' St Aubyn, Major Jim Barr USAF, Flt Lt Pete Ginger. Flg Off. John Blackley, junior engineering officer. XR765 first flew on 10 November 1965 and was issued to 5 Squadron on 8 March 1966. It was modified to F.6 in 1967 and allocated to 23 Squadron on 25 March 1968, subsequently serving with 11 and 5 Squadrons at Binbrook. XR765 was lost on 2 July 1981 during Exercise *Priory* when it crashed into the sea thirty miles east of Spurn Head after a double reheat fire. Flt Lt J.G. Wild of 5 Squadron ejected safely. (*Brian Allchin*)

Left: F.6 XS920/L of 74 'Tiger' Squadron on a *Tambour* cross-country from Leuchars with a Victor K.1A tanker in winter 1967 as a prelude to the squadron's deployment to Malaya that summer. The loss of the Valiant tanker fleet in 1965 resulted in a rapid conversion of Victor B.1 bombers to K.1A in-flight refuelling tankers, the first flying on 28 April 1965. F.6 XS920 first flew on 25 October 1966 and was issued to 'Tiger' Squadron on 5 December that year. It was transferred to 11 Squadron in August 1970 and entered service with 5 Squadron in November 1983. XS920 was lost on 13 July 1984 during ACM when it hit power cables and crashed at Heuslingen, twenty-five miles east of Bremen, West Germany, while following a USAF A-10 at 200 ft. Flt Lt Dave 'Jack' Frost was killed. In June 1967, thirteen of 74 Squadron's F.6s transferred from the UK to Tengah, Singapore, in Operation *Hydraulic*, the longest and largest in-flight refuelling operation hitherto flown, staging through Akrotiri, Masirah, and Gan, and using seventeen Victor tankers from Marham, for a four-year tour of duty in the FEAF (Far East Air Force). (*Jimmy Jewell*)

Below: Two Lightnings of 74 'Tiger' Squadron making a night take-off at RAF Tengah, Singapore in 1968. (*Jimmy Jewell*)

Tiger Taking off from Tengah. F.6 XR771/D of 74 Squadron getting airborne from RAF Tengah, Singapore in 1968. (*Dave Roome*)

'A' Flight Detachment, 74 'Tiger' Squadron, at RAAF Butterworth, Malaya, in February 1968. The nearest aircraft is XR771/D, which is now on display at the Midland Air Museum in Coventry. XS927/N was last flown in October 1986 and was scrapped in 1988. XS895/H was finally scrapped in April 1988. (*Jimmy Jewell*)

Lightnings of 74 'Tiger' Squadron at rest at Tengah, Singapore in 1968. (*Dave Roome*)

Above: F.1A XM188/F of 11 Squadron had a premature end at Coltishall on 21 June 1968. Sqn Ldr Arthur Tilsley taxied this aircraft in with no brakes and crashed it into the side of 1 Hangar at the station. One Avon jammed at about 80% power and a Rolls-Royce technician scrambled underneath to the engine bay and eventually managed to stop the runaway engine. Arthur Tilsley, meanwhile, had climbed out of the cockpit onto the roof of the hangar offices. (*David Grimer*)

Opposite: The Lightnings' *raison d'être* was to intercept the high-flying Soviet bombers that approached British and NATO air space. In both the UK and Germany the Lightning was kept in a permanent state of high readiness, called Quick Reaction Alert (QRA) in the UK, and Battle Flight in Germany. In the UK the readiness state was ten minutes and in Germany it was five minutes. This Lightning, shadowing a Soviet Bear over the North Sea in July 1968, is a 23 Squadron F.6 from Leuchars, Scotland. (*Bruce Hopkins*)

Above: Lightning Line-Up. 226 OCU's Lightnings at Coltishall late in 1968. (*Ken Hazell*)

Left: F.3 XP750 of 111 Squadron crossing the Suffolk coast in 1968, inbound for Wattisham. This Lightning first flew on 3 January 1964 and was issued to AFDS before joining 'Treble-One' two days before Christmas 1965. After a spell with 56 Squadron and 60 MU, XP750 rejoined 'Treble-One' in September 1968. It went on to serve in 23 Squadron, from 15 May 1974 to 20 October 1975, the LTF, and finally, in the eighties, 5 Squadron, at Binbrook, before being used as a decoy from September 1987 and scrapped. (*Dick Bell*)

Above: T.55 55-711/A (G-27-70), one of the production batch of six two-seaters for the Royal Saudi Air Force, at Coltishall for Saudi pilot training with 226 OCU. First flown on 29 August 1967, 55-711 operated from the Norfolk station from 2 February 1968 until the end of August 1968. It was then flown to Saudi Arabia and re-serialised 55-71, operated with the Saudi LCU (Lightning Conversion Unit), and 6, 13 and 2 Squadrons before returning to Warton as ZF597 in January 1986. (*David Grimer*)

Right: 55-711/A, 55-713/C, which arrived at Coltishall on 2 February 1968, and 55-714/D, which arrived on 22 March, on a formation sortie along the Norfolk coast. 55-711/A and 55-713/C were flown to Saudi Arabia on 27 August 1969. On 11 July 1969 55-714/D was flown to Saudi Arabia via Akrotiri, Cyprus, by Al Love. (*Via Mike Hobson*)

Saudi T.54 T-birds, 55-712/B and 55-714/D at Coltishall in 1968. 55-712 first flew on 12 October 1967 and was received by the RSAF at Jedda on 11 July 1969. It served with the LCU and 6 squadron, crashing into Half Moon Bay on 21 May 1974. 55-714 first flew on 1 February 1968 and was also received by the RSAF on 11 July 1969. After service with the RSAF, it returned to Warton (as ZF595) on 22 January 1986. (*Graham Mitchell*)

T-birds taxiing. These two T.5s of 226 OCU taxi past the tower at Coltishall in May 1969. XS452, leading, first flew on 30 June 1965, joined 226 OCU on 20 September that year and continued to operate from 'Colt' until February 1971 when, after overhaul at 60 MU, it was allocated to 'Treble-One' Squadron. After many years' faithful service '452' was SOC. in June 1988 and was one of the Lightnings purchased by Arnold Glass, being flown to Cranfield by John Aldington on 29 June 1988. At the time, few would have believed that XS452 would ever fly again. However, on 9 March 1999, this T-bird, now registered ZU-BBD, and the first of four of Mike Beachy Head's Lightnings in his growing family of jets in the Thunder City operation, roared along the runway at South Africa's Cape Town International Airport in the hands of Keith Hartley and Mike Beachy Head. Thunder City's three other flyable Lightnings are T.5 ZU-BEX (XS451) and F.6s ZU-BEY (XP693) and ZU-BEW (XR773). (*Dick Bell*)

F.1A XM214 of 226 OCU over Norfolk in July 1969. This
Lightning first flew on 29 June 1961 and was issued to 111
Squadron on 1 August. On 4 August 1965, XM214 joined 226
OCU and was finally withdrawn from active OCU use by June
1974. In 1974 XM214 went to RAF Gütersloh as an airfield
decoy aircraft. (*Dick Bell*)

XN776 was built as an F.2 and first flew on 18 October 1962. It was issued to 19 Squadron on 13 February 1963 and received the code letter 'E' (pictured here during a visit to Coltishall). In January 1969 XN776 was converted to F.2A by BAC at Warton and reissued to 19 Squadron, where it now received the code letter 'C'. XN776 flew operationally for the last time on 3 March 1977 and was used at Leuchars as a decoy. XN776 is now displayed at the Museum of Flight at East Fortune in Scotland. (*Adrian Savage*)

T for two. T-birds T.4 XM994 and XM996 of 226 OCU at Coltishall over Norfolk in November 1969. XM994 first flew on 12 March 1962 and was issued to 19 Squadron at Leconfield on 6 November 1962. After being used to help conversion of both 19 and 92 Squadrons to Lightnings, XM994 was transferred to 226 OCU at Coltishall on 27 June 1963, where it served until 8 May 1974. The aircraft was scrapped in 1977. XM996 first flew on 13 April 1962 and was issued to the LCS at Middleton St George on 29 January 1963. It operated with 226 OCU from 1 June 1963 until June 1974, when it was withdrawn from use, and was finally scrapped after being used for fire practice at Manston. (*Dick Bell*)

Right: T.5 XV328/Z of 29 Squadron. This T-bird first flew on 22 December 1966 and was issued to 29 Squadron in March 1967. It was badly damaged in October 1969 while on detachment at Coltishall. Repaired, it rejoined 29 Squadron in February 1970, when this beautiful climbing shot was taken by Flt Lt (later Sqn Ldr) Dick Bell. XV328 subsequently went on to serve with 5 and 11 Squadrons and the LTF at Binbrook. In June 1968 it was one of several Lightnings purchased by Arnold Glass and based at Cranfield. (*Dick Bell*)

Below: 'Linies' of 29 Squadron are seen in special white overalls (which are always worn by groundcrew handling aircraft flown by air vice-marshals and above) at Wattisham in February 1970. It is probably apocryphal, but folklore has it that 29 Squadron's 'three-X' marking was the result of the originator being told to paint two Xs, followed by 'one X'. For twenty-nine it should, of course, have read 'XXIX'! (*Dick Bell*)

Sqn Ldr Sam Lucas, 29 Squadron's 'aeros' pilot, climbs into the cockpit of F.3 XP763/P. Lucas was an exceptional solo aerobatic display pilot, having flown with the *Firebirds* in 1963 while seconded to 111 Squadron. He was also an 'ad-libber' who would often get 'bored' with his show and throw in some unannounced routines! XP763, which first flew on 11 September 1964, was issued to 23 Squadron in July 1966. After service with 56 Squadron, XP763 joined 29 Squadron in October 1967 and was coded 'G'. Returning from 60 MU in 1969, it was recoded 'P', and it finally ended its days on the Wattisham fire dump following its retirement at the end of 1974. (*Dick Bell*)

F.6 XS931/G of 11 Squadron first flew on 31 March 1967 and joined the Squadron on 31 May 1967. It was put into store in July 1976 and by December 1977 had joined 5 Squadron, coded 'D'. On 25 May 1979 Flg Off. Pete Coker took XS931 off from Binbrook, but was forced to abandon the sortie near Flamborough Head when he suffered control restriction, which was later determined to have been caused by Foreign Object Damage (FOD). Coker ejected successfully and XS931 crashed into the sea off Hornsea. (*Dick Bell*)

Toting a pair of Firestreak missiles, F.3 XP698/B of 29 Squadron is seen plugged into a Houchin ground power set at Akrotiri, Cyprus during the Squadron's annual missile practice camp, arriving on the Mediterranean island on 23 February 1970. XP698 first flew on 28 August 1963. On 16 February 1972, XP698 and F.3 XP747 collided off Harwich during a 29 Squadron sortie. Flt Lt Paul Cooper, the pilot of XP698, was killed. Flt Lt Paul Reynolds ejected safely from XP747. (*Dick Bell*)

F.3 XP756/E of 29 Squadron *en route* to Cyprus on 2 March 1970, one of five of the Squadron's Lightnings sent to join three that had arrived at Akrotiri on 23 February. At the controls is the Boss, Wg Cdr Brian Carroll, who commanded 29 Squadron from October 1969 to July 1971. A ninth Lightning, T.5 XV329/Z, followed the second flight in on 3 March. The Lightnings' journey from Wattisham to Cyprus saw them refuel no less than six times in the F.3 and ten (!) in the T.5. T-birds were often taken on detachment to Cyprus to familiarise new pilots with the procedures involved in performing successful target interceptions. XP756 first flew on 22 June 1964. It suffered a bad engine fire in 1970, and was lost on 25 January 1971 when it crashed into the North Sea off Great Yarmouth after a reheat fire. Captain William 'Bill' R. Povilus USAF, who was attached to 29 Squadron, ejected safely and was picked up by a USAF 'Jolly Green Giant' from Woodbridge. Povilus, who had flown 373 combat missions as a forward air controller in Vietnam, had been attached to 29 Squadron since 1969. (*Dick Bell*)

Left: F.3s XP706/F and XP761/N of 'Treble-One' Squadron in formation with F-104G Starfighters FX-83, flown by Major Andre Richir, OC 1 Wing at Beauvechain/Bevekom, and FX-27, flown by Cpn Jean-Pierre Gilson, both of 350-ème (*escadrille/smaldeel*–squadron, or *ème*), 1 Wing, of the *Force Aérienne Belge (FAé)/Belgische Luchtmacht (BLu)* at Beauvechain/Bevekom, over Belgium on 5 May 1970. They were photographed by ADC (Warrant Officer) Jan Govaerts from the back seat of TF-104G FC-05 from 1 Wing, flown by Cpn Marcel Vanderstockt. 111 Squadron paid an exchange visit to 1 Wing during 28 April–6 May 1970. XP706/F first flew on 28 October 1963 and was issued to 74 'Tiger' Squadron on 13 July 1964. XP761/N first flew on 26 August 1964 and was issued to 23 Squadron on 27 October (and is still sporting that squadron's tail letter; it was later changed to 'Z'). Coincidentally, both these Belgian Starfighters ended their careers in one piece although they had mishaps along the way. In 1973 FX-83 suffered a heavy nose-shimmy after blowing a nose-wheel tyre on landing at Beauvechain. It was repaired and was used later by the *Slivers* aerobatic team. Early in its career, on 9 July 1964, FX-27 suffered a lightning strike at Court St Etienne! This aircraft joined the Turkish Air Force in August 1983. After being used as decoys, F.3 XP706 was finally scrapped late in 1987, and F.3 XP761 was burnt on 10 November 1986. (*Jan Govaerts*)

Above: Flt Lts Hood and Bell run in over Wattisham in close formation. This view of the port side of XP763/P reveals fin 'zaps' from Dutch F-104G unit, 322 Squadron at Leeuwarden, and a French Mirage III *escadrille*. (*Dick Bell*)

Opposite: F.3 XP763/P is brought in close to Flt Lt Dick Bell's camera high over East Anglia on a hazy summer's day in 1970 by Flt Lt Pete Hood. This Lightning, which first flew on 11 September 1964, has recently returned from Cyprus, as the panel covering the AVPIN (isopropylnitrate) starter fuel tank is still painted white. This was done to reduce the temperature inside the tank, thus preventing the AVPIN from evaporating. XP763 was issued to 23 Squadron in July 1966 and transferred to 56 Squadron early in 1967. It was assigned to 29 Squadron in October the same year, serving until December 1974 when it was put into store at Wattisham. XP763 was SOC and scrapped in March 1975. (*Dick Bell*)

Remarkable take-off shot in 1971 of a fellow 29 Squadron Lightning by Sqn Ldr Dick Bell. The nose-wheel is still spinning from the take-off run at RAF Wattisham. (*Dick Bell*)

Line-up of 19 Squadron F.2As in March 1971. (*Brian Allchin*)

F.3 XP764/C of 29 Squadron thumps down onto the runway at Wattisham in 1972. XP764 first flew on 19 September 1964 and was issued to 74 Squadron on 3 November that year. It joined 29 Squadron (as 'E') in July 1967, and it was recoded 'C' in September 1969, remaining until 30 October 1972 when XP764 was transferred to 5 Squadron. XP764 finished its days as a decoy aircraft in 1987 and was scrapped late that year. (*Pete Nash*)

F.3 XP746/J of 111 Squadron overshoots at Wattisham and goes round again. This aircraft first flew on 26 March 1964 and was issued to 56 Squadron on 12 November 1969. It joined 'Treble-One' Squadron on 4 August 1970 and operated for four years before going into store at Wattisham in October 1974. XP746 was SOC in April 1975 and was used as a target (Proof and Experimental Establishment (PEE)) aircraft for gunnery at Shoeburyness in 1976. (*Pete Nash*)

Left: And now for something completely different! F.1A XM177 of the Wattisham TFF. This Lightning served the unit between 23 April and September 1971, when the picture was taken, and again between May 1972 and 14 September 1973. XM177 first flew on 20 December 1960 and was first issued to 56 Squadron in March 1963. This Lightning, which also served in 226 OCU, Leuchars TFF, and 23 Squadron, was scrapped in 1974. (*Dick Bell*)

Below: F.2A XN733/Y of 19 Squadron refuelling from Victor tanker XH651 of 57 Squadron in 1971. XN733 first flew on 1 February 1962 and was issued to 92 Squadron on 6 June 1963. It suffered a Cat. 4 starter explosion in 1968 and was transported by road to Warton for repairs. After conversion to F.2A, on 31 December 1969, XN733 was issued to 19 Squadron, and coded 'R'. On 18 June 1970 the aircraft was used by BAC and took part in the September 1970 Society of British Aerospace Constructors (SBAC) show at Farnborough. After a spell at 60 MU, XN733 joined 92 Squadron in October 1970 and was coded 'U'. It became 'Y' with 19 Squadron at Laarbruch from December 1970. (*Brian Allchin*)

F.2A XN786/M of 19 Squadron landing at Gütersloh in March 1971. This aircraft was built as an F.2 and first flew on 12 February 1963 before being issued to 92 Squadron on 9 April 1963. After conversion to F.2A standard, XN786 joined 19 Squadron on 1 July 1969. It was badly damaged in a ground fire at Gütersloh on 4 August 1976. (*Brian Allchin*)

Above: Sixteen from Nineteen. F.2s of 19 Squadron formate over Gütersloh, on 13 July 1971, led by Wg Cdr Les Davies. (*Brian Allchin*)

Left: F.2As of 19 Squadron in formation. XN776/C, the nearest aircraft to the cockpit, joined 19 Squadron on 13 August 1969. It last flew, in 92 Squadron, on 3 March 1977, and finished its RAF career as a decoy at RAF Leuchars. It is now preserved at the Museum of Flight at East Fortune, Scotland. To its left is XN777K, which joined 19 Squadron on 26 March 1968. It transferred to 92 Squadron in January 1977 and on 6 April was declared non-operational and issued to RAF Wildenrath as a decoy. (*Brian Allchin*)

Above: F.2As of 19 Squadron tighten up formation. The nearest Lightning is XN790 which was built as an F.2 and first flew on 20 March 1963 before being issued to 92 Squadron, coded 'E' (later 'K'), on 25 April. XN790/K went to BAC on 26 June 1968 for conversion to F.2A, and was reissued to 19 Squadron, as 'L' on 30 January 1969. XN790 became a decoy at Laarbruch on New Year's Eve 1976. (*Brian Allchin*)

Right: 74 Squadron disbanded at Tengah on 25 August 1971 and, starting on 2 September 1971, all remaining F.6s were flown on the 6,000-mile, 13-hour trip to Akrotiri, Cyprus, staging through Gan and Muharraq and completing seven in-flight refuellings with Victor tankers, for transfer to 56 Squadron. XR773/F, here flown by Flt Lt Dave Roome, is fitted with overwing tanks, or 'overburgers', for the flight on 6 September 1971 from Tengah to Gan. XR773 flew for the first time on 28 February 1966. It is now one of four Lightnings on the strength of the Thunder City fleet in Cape Town, South Africa. (*Dave Roome*)

Up periscope. Remarkable view of a 74 'Tiger' Squadron Lightning through the periscope of a Victor tanker during an air-to-air refuelling on the ferry flight from Tengah to Cyprus in September 1971. (*Jimmy Jewell*)

F.6s XS921/M and XR761/B of 74 Squadron during the stopover at Gan in September 1971. XS921 first flew on 17 November 1966 and was issued to the *Tigers* on 21 December that year. After delivery to Cyprus and service with 56 Squadron, XS921 served with 5 and 11 Squadrons. It was lost on 19 September 1985 when it crashed thirty miles off Flamborough Head after an uncontrolled spin. Flt Lt Craig Penrice, the pilot, ejected but he suffered severe leg injuries. XR761, which first flew on 30 September 1965, suffered a similar fate on 8 November 1984 with 5 Squadron. (*John Hale*)

F.6 XR725/A touching down at Gan after the flight from Tengah. This Lightning, which was built as an F.3, first flew on 19 February 1965, and was issued to 23 Squadron after conversion to F.6, on 16 August 1967. It suffered a taxiing accident while on detachment to Sola, Norway, on 26 October, was flown home and repaired at 60 MU, and on 28 August 1968 was one of two F.6s which made the non-stop, air-refuelled, 7 hr 20 min flight to Goose Bay, Canada, to appear in an air show at Toronto. It was flown there, and back on 3 September, by Sqn Ldr Ed Durham, and on its return, was put into store. XR725 joined 74 Squadron in July 1970. After serving with the *Tigers* and, subsequently, with 56 Squadron, XR725 operated with 5 and 11 Squadrons, and the LTF, logging a career total of 3,870.20 hours' flying time, before being scrapped in 1988. (*John Hale*)

Left: F.6s XR761/B and XS921/M refuelling from a Marham-based Victor *en route* to Cyprus. XS921 was coded 'Q' with 56 Squadron and served the *Firebirds* until the summer of 1974, joining 11 Squadron as 'L' on 2 August. (*Mike Rigg*)

Below: XR761/B, which became 'B' in 56 Squadron, served the *Firebirds* until the summer of 1976, when, after overhaul at 60 MU, it was transferred to Binbrook where it served both 11 and 5 Squadrons. On 8 November 1984 XR761/AC crashed into the North Sea eight miles east of Spurn Head following pitch trimmer failure after take-off. Both reheat fire warning lights then came on, indicating that both No. 1 and No. 2 engines were on fire. Flt Lt Mike D. Hale, the pilot, burned-off fuel, intending to land back at Binbrook but smoke and fire caused him to eject. Hale was picked up after twenty-five minutes in the sea. (*Mike Rigg*)

'SCRAMBLE! SCRAMBLE! SCRAMBLE!' Three F.2As of 19 Squadron getting airborne at Gütersloh, September 1971. Sqn Ldr Tony Paxton, a 19 Squadron pilot at Gütersloh in the early seventies, recalls: '*QRA, or, in RAF Germany, Battle Flight, meant that from the alert, normally a bell or a siren, one or both of the Lightnings in the alert facility had to be airborne within the prescribed time by day or night in all weathers. The pilots on the RAF Germany squadrons would be rostered to hold the Battle Flight duty for a twenty-four-hour period every week or so* (ground crew could stay for a week at a time – all living in accommodation just a few feet from their aircraft in the Q shed). *It was a popular duty because one was almost certain to get a training scramble during each period and always had the next day off.*

The reason for the frequent training scrambles was that five minutes really is not very long to run to an aeroplane, climb the ladder, strap in, start engines, taxi to the runway and take off. If one were asleep when the bell sounded the time allowed was even tighter. Of course, there were several live scrambles each year; they would normally be because of East German/Soviet activity near to the border, unidentified radar contacts or even suspected aerial smugglers.' (Brian Allchin)

F.1 XM144 of the Leuchars TFF on a visit to RAF Wattisham, Suffolk, in January 1972. This Lightning first flew on 14 March 1960 and saw extensive service with several units before joining the Scottish unit on 30 July 1971. It last flew on 7 November 1973 and was used as a decoy at Leuchars until it was refurbished in 1979 for gate guard duty as 'J' of 74 'Tiger' Squadron. (*Pete Nash*)

One can almost feel the cold in this wintertime shot at
Leconfield early in 1972 as a Lightning gets airborne. (*Dick Bell*)

F.2A XN773/E of 92 Squadron dumps its parachute on landing at Leconfield in 1972. XN773 was built as an F.2 and first flew on 13 June 1962. It was originally operated by Aeroplane Armament Experimental Establishment (A&AEE), and Rolls-Royce at Hucknall, before passing, in turn, to 33 MU and 60 MU. In 1967 XN773 was converted to F.2A standard at BAC Warton, being issued to 92 Squadron as 'E' on 26 June 1968. (*Dick Bell*)

XN773/E and XN791/D of 92 Squadron in flight over Germany. Like XN773, XN791 was also built as an F.2 and first flew on 4 April 1963. It was the last Lightning in 'Shiny Blue' to have a blue fin. Red and yellow chequers were applied in 1968 and were used until late in 1971 when blue was removed from fin and spine. In 1972 olive green camouflage overall was applied to Lightnings in RAF Germany. With disbandment of 92 Squadron on 31 March 1977, both aircraft were withdrawn from use and used as decoys. (*John Bryant*)

55-411/G-27-79/B, the second of the two T.55s for the Kuwaiti Air Force, in Kuwait in March 1972. This aircraft first flew on 3 April 1969. 55-411 was flown to Kuwait via Akrotiri, Cyprus, and Jedda in Saudi Arabia (with 53-423) on 3 December 1969 by Flt Lt Adcock and Sqn Ldr Hopkins. (*Peter Hayward*)

Two of the Kuwaiti Air Force's F.53 Lightnings undergoing maintenance in a hangar in Kuwait in March 1972. (*Peter Hayward*)

A continuing problem with the Lightning was fuel and hydraulic fires. The two engines, No. 2 mounted above and No. 1 behind the missile pack, had long jet pipes close to the external skin. In an attempt to solve some of the in-flight fire problems 29 Squadron's XS459/T was loaned to BAC in spring 1972 for trials, though it remained with the squadron. The safety equipment was removed from the right-hand seat and small reservoirs of blue dye were strategically placed around the airframe. A control box operated by the BAC test pilot took the place of the safety equipment and the fuselage was painted with white distemper so that the dye trails could clearly be seen. XS459 is now on display at Wellesley Aviation at Narborough, Norfolk. (*Pete Nash*)

Clean Mk. 2. F.2 XN779/X of 19 Squadron, RAF Germany, May 1972. XN779 first flew on 20 November 1962 and joined 19 Squadron on 27 March 1963 as 'G'. This aircraft was withdrawn from use in August 1973, and used for spares. (*Brian Allchin*)

T.4 XM973 at 60 MU Leconfield in July 1972. This aircraft first flew on 17 May 1961 and was used for twenty-seven development flights at Warton before being issued to AFDS on 3 August 1962. In spring 1963 this T-bird was loaned to 74 'Tiger' Squadron at Coltishall, and to 'Treble-One' Squadron at Wattisham. It left 60 MU on 29 September 1972 as XM973/V of 19 Squadron, finishing its days as a decoy aircraft at Bruggen. Behind XM973 is F.2 XN794/W of 19 Squadron. This Lightning first flew on 16 May 1963 and was damaged by fire on its second engine run. After repairs at 33 MU in September 1963, XN794 was issued to 92 Squadron and coded 'P'. XN794 was withdrawn in 1973 and used as a decoy at Gütersloh. (*Dick Bell*)

Left: F.6 XS901/T of 56 Squadron fitted with overwing tanks, on a test flight from Leconfield in 1972 (XS901 was the last aircraft to pass through 60 MU, which carried out all major Lightning servicing after the closure of 33 MU at Lyneham in August 1966). XS901 first flew on 1 July 1966 and was issued to 5 Squadron in February 1967. In February 1972 it was allocated to 56 Squadron, serving with the *Firebirds* until 1 July 1976. XS901 went on to serve with 11 and 5 Squadrons before being used as a Battle Damage Repair (BDR) aircraft at Bruggen in May 1988. (*Dick Bell*)

Below: Exciting Lightning. F.6 getting airborne from 60 MU at Leconfield in 1972. (*Dick Bell*)

Above: Two F.6s of 5 Squadron, their brake chutes billowing, taxi in after landing on the wet runway at Leconfield after a spring shower. (*Dick Bell*)

Right: Blue Moon. (*Dick Bell*)

Left: F.3 XR749/Q of 5 Squadron pictured in the early seventies by Tony Paxton. This Lightning first flew on 30 April 1965 and after being partly modified to F.6 was then de-modified, and issued to 56 Squadron on 30 October 1967. It joined 5 Squadron on 21 November 1972. (*Tony Paxton*)

Below: F.3 XR749/Q tanking from Victor K.1 XA939 of 214 Squadron. XR749 later operated with 11 Squadron and the LTF, before being used for Battle Damage Repair (BDR) duties at Leuchars after making an emergency landing there on 17 February 1987 while *en route* to Lossiemouth. (*Tony Paxton*)

Bear in the Air. High above the North Sea on 15 September 1972, one of the Soviet's long-range reconnaissance aircraft is intercepted and shadowed by F.6 XR753/A flown by Sqn Ldr Bruce Hopkins, CO of 23 Squadron, from Leuchars. The photo was taken from a Phantom of 43 Squadron also stationed at Leuchars. XR753 was built as an F.3A and first flew on 23 June 1965. It joined 23 Squadron on 10 August 1967 and operated with them (coded 'V') until March 1968 when it was converted to F.6, and again, from 21 August 1971 to late 1975 (as 'A'). After further service late in its career with 11 and 5 Squadrons, XR753 finally became a BDR aircraft in May 1988. (*MoD*)

Easy does it! (*Tony Paxton*)

Fill her up! (*Tony Paxton*)

F.6 XR726/N of 5 Squadron. Note the Day-Glo Maltese Cross 'zap' on the fin. This Lightning was built as an F.3 and first flew on 26 February 1965 before being converted to F.6 and being issued to 60 MU where it was used by the station flight. It joined 5 Squadron on 29 February 1968 after first being loaned to 23 Squadron, and was damaged by a No. 2 engine starter fire at Binbrook on 19 October 1973. XR726 later joined 23 Squadron and on 15 August 1979 lost a rudder in flight, but managed to land safely. After further service – and no further mishaps – with 5 and 11 Squadrons and the LTF, XR7236 was withdrawn from use in July 1987 and stripped for spares. (*Tony Paxton*)

On the night of 31 January 1973 Captain Gary Catren, a USAF exchange officer attached to 226 OCU, with student pilot Flt Lt George Smith, attempted a take-off for an SCT (Staff Continuation Training) sortie in T.5 XS420 from Runway 04 at Coltishall, but the lower reheat failed to ignite. With flaps down (as per a Command directive!), the resultant force of the upper reheat did not allow the nosewheel to be raised. As the T-bird headed for the barrier, Catren, a Texan, shouted, 'Sheeeeeeeet, George!' Smith, wrongly believing his instructor was calling for the chute, dutifully pulled the brake-chute handle, only for the chute to disintegrate into cinders in the reheat! XS420 took the barrier with it into the overshoot but the T-bird fortunately dug in before it crashed into the railway line near the base, and both pilots walked away unhurt. XS420 flew for the last time in May 1983. It is now displayed at the Fenland Aviation Museum in Wisbech. (*Via Dick Doleman*)

Opposite, top: Lightning leaving. June 1973. (*Dick Bell*)

T.5 XS417/Z of 23 Squadron at RAF Leuchars in July 1973. XS417 was the first production T.5 to fly, on 17 July 1964. It was used for forty-seven flights in development flying and was first issued to 226 OCU at Coltishall on 25 May 1965. XS417 then joined 23 Squadron in February 1966 where it was coded 'Z'. Between October 1970 and April 1971 XS417 was loaned back to the OCU. After a spell with 56 Squadron in 1975 'Z' went on to serve with the LTF, 11 Squadron, and finally, from March 1983, the LTF. On 13 March 1984 this T-bird was damaged when its ventral tank scraped the runway on take-off. Repaired, it flew on until April 1987 when it was finally withdrawn from use. XS417 was scrapped in March 1988. (*Bruce Hopkins*)

Opposite, bottom: Flaming June. Lightning getting airborne. (*Dick Bell*)

Four Spitfires and two Hurricanes of the Battle of Britain Memorial Flight (BBMF) overfly T.5 XS449 of 226 OCU at Coltishall, the famous Battle of Britain fighter station in Norfolk, in October 1973. The BBMF, which was formed at RAF Biggin Hill as the Historic Aircraft Flight on 11 July 1957 with three Spitfires and one Hurricane, operated from Coltishall from 1964 to 1976. XS449 first flew on 30 April 1965 and was issued to the OCU on 17 July that year. It was loaned out to 74 'Tiger' Squadron at Coltishall during summer and autumn 1966 and, in March 1969, was damaged while flying through a thunderstorm. In September 1974 XS449 was put into store and in November 1975 became a decoy before being scrapped in 1987. (*Via Dave Seward*)

F.3 XR715 first flew on 14 November 1964 and was issued to 'Treble-One' Squadron on 8 January 1965, but after joining 29 Squadron in 1970 its career was dramatically cut short, when on 13 February 1974 XR715/R was abandoned after an Engine Change Unit (ECU) fire. Flt Lt Terence 'Taff' A. Butcher of 29 Squadron ejected safely and suffered no ill effects, flying again the next day! XR715/R, meanwhile, crashed at Watermill Farm, Mellis, near Halesworth. This remarkable shot shows the fire being extinguished by firemen of the Suffolk Fire Brigade, who were quickly on the scene. (*Via Ritchie Pymar*)

F.6 XS936/B of 23 Squadron at Leuchars, Fife, Scotland, in March 1974. XS936 first flew on 31 May 1967 and was issued to 23 Squadron on 18 August 1967. On 28 August 1968 it was one of two F.6s which made the non-stop, air-refuelled, 7 hr 20 min flight to Goose Bay, Canada, as a reserve Lightning to XR725/A, flown by Sqn Ldr Ed Durham, which appeared in an air show at Toronto. XS936/B was flown to Canada, and back on 3 September, by Flt Lt Geoff Brindle. This aircraft entered the Binbrook store in November 1975 and thereafter continued to serve 11 and 5 Squadrons, and the LTF. XS936 last flew in October 1987 and was scrapped in April 1988 after logging a total of 3,961.50 hours' flying time during its career. (*Bruce Hopkins*)

Snake charmer? During 1974 when Flg Off. (now Sqn Ldr) Clive Rowley was flying F.2As from Gütersloh with 19 Squadron, he was photographed with this tanker hose coiled like a snake. Clive explains: *'We didn't get much tanking practice as Germany-based squadrons – spookily enough the tankers were only available on Fridays, meaning that the crews had to stop at the weekend!*

On about my sixth-ever tanking sortie (with gaps of several weeks between each), I think I was probably getting overconfident about this 'tricky' skill and when I attempted to connect with the hose trailed from this particular Victor tanker I used all the wrong techniques, including looking at the "basket" just before connecting. Seeing that I was going to miss to the right I put on a large "bootfull" of left rudder to slide my probe into the "basket". Unfortunately the probe tip "rimmed" the "basket", didn't engage and pushed it sideways. As I backed off I was surprised and horrified to see a very large lateral "whip" develop in the tanker hose which grew as it snaked towards the HDU (pod) and grew further as it snaked back towards me. Next thing my Lightning was "clobbered" by this hose with a life of its own, there was a loud bang as it hit me somewhere on the intake and my aircraft was tipped ninety degrees of bank towards the Victor's fuselage – rather frightening!

I levelled the aircraft to straight and level and having achieved this and averted any collision risk I was appalled to see that the hose – all fifty-five feet of it – had fallen off, over Germany! I transmitted, "Tanker Call-sign, your hose has fallen off!" This didn't go down well! A visual inspection by my leader reported possible damage to the intake.

After a slow-speed handling check I landed back at Gütersloh safely. Unfortunately, the stainless steel double skin of my intake had been dented and the skins squashed together. They were talking about several months to repair it. I was not popular.

Meanwhile, I spent the weekend worrying about the tanker hose. Had it, for example, caused a multiple pile-up on an autobahn with significant loss of life? No news was good news, but the aircraft damage was still threatening the previously good relationship with the Boss.

BAe Warton sent an expert panel beater called "Ted", and his expertise saved the day (and my "bacon"). My "punishment" was to buy "Ted" lots of beer, present him with a framed picture of the aircraft and have my photograph taken with a Victor hose wrapped around me. The hose was found some weeks later in a German farmer's field and returned to us – unfortunately! So you see it was a punishment!'

With over 6,000 hours of flying time, Clive is currently a specialist aircrew instructor with 56 (R) Squadron and one of the five fighter pilots in the BBMF, at Coningsby. (*Tony Paxton*)

Above: F.6s of 23 Squadron taking off from Leuchars in 1974. (*Bruce Hopkins*)

Right: Four F.6s XS927/O, XS937/C, XR770/L, XS935/J, of 23 Squadron in line abreast on a sortie from Leuchars in 1974. XS927 first flew on 15 February 1967 and joined 23 Squadron after first serving with 74 Squadron. This aircraft was last flown in October 1986 and was scrapped by April 1988. XS937 first flew on 26 June 1967 and was issued to 23 Squadron on 21 August. It later joined 11 Squadron and was lost off Flamborough Head on 30 July 1976 when the starboard under-carriage failed to lower and was trailed at twenty degrees. Flg Off. Simon C.C. 'Much' Manning ejected safely at 7,000 ft and 300 knots. XR770/L first flew on 16 December 1965 and was allocated to 23 Squadron in May 1972 after first being issued to 74 Squadron in 1966. It last flew on 29 April 1988 and was dis-mantled for display in Grimsby. XS935 first flew on 29 May 1967 and was issued to 23 Squadron on 5 January 1968. It was finally scrapped in 1988. (*Bruce Hopkins*)

Above: F.2A XN781 'Bravo' of 19 Squadron, RAF Germany in November 1974. The Boss's aircraft (Wg Cdr, later Air Cdre, Robert 'Bob' Barcillon), it is being flown by Flt Lt Clive Rowley. This aircraft had, for some time, carried the 'Top Cat' symbol on the side (a stencil of a cat's rear) with the inscription 'Top Cat, Often Licked, Never Beaten!' When Bob Barcillon took over the Squadron in mid-1974 he was, unbeknown to him, nicknamed 'The Pink Panther' by the groundcrew. When the Pink Panther emblem also appeared, overnight, above the RAF roundel, facing backwards and holding the Wg Cdr's pennant (which was, of course, already in place), the cat was, quite literally, out of the bag! (*Tony Paxton*)

Right: F.2A XN733/Y of 19 Squadron in December 1974, now wearing the matt, dark-olive-green camouflage applied to the upper surfaces of the RAF Germany Lightnings from 1972. XN733 was finally withdrawn from service in January 1977 and used as a decoy at Laarbruch. (*Tony Paxton*)

Opposite: F.2A XN771/P of 19 Squadron eight miles over West Germany on combat air patrol in spring 1975. Tony Paxton recalls: '*Very early one summer Sunday morning in the early seventies I was fast asleep in the Battle Flight "shed" at Gütersloh when a loud ringing noise penetrated through my dreams. Because of the very short reaction time, we used to sleep in full flying kit including anti-G suit and boots, the life jacket was hanging over the Firestreak missile on the aircraft and the flying helmet was plugged into the oxygen hose and radio lead and perched on top of the canopy arch.*

Once the full meaning of the bell ringing in my ears had sunk in I was up and running, colliding with the ground crew, in various stages of undress, who were also running to perform their tasks to get the Lightning airborne in the shortest possible time. I arrived at the aeroplane and after donning the life jacket I did up a couple of buttons as I scrambled up the ladder. Once in the cockpit with my helmet on, one of the lads was right there handing me the straps as my hands moved around the switch panels, readying the aircraft for start as I checked in on the telebrief (a secure landline communication to the base operations and the sector controller) and declared myself "On State".

Once I was strapped in, the ground crew removed the safety pins from the ejection seat and the canopy, and the ground power was plugged in. The mighty Lightning was sitting there, fully armed with all the electrical systems running. We just awaited the order to launch. That order came immediately . . . "Vector 070. Climb Angels 10. Contact Crabtree [code name for an air defence radar site manned by the German Air Force]. SCRAMBLE! SCRAMBLE! SCRAMBLE!"

Even before the sector controller had said the word, one engine was running and the second was already winding up as I acknowledged the instructions. The aircraft rolled forward and the external power leads pulled out of the aircraft sockets automatically as I lowered the canopy. The taxiway was just long enough for me to complete the pre-take-off checks before pointing the great machine straight down the mile-and-a-half long runway, lighting the reheats and thundering into the sky.

As soon as we were airborne I retracted the undercarriage, pulled into a tight climbing turn, and looked at my watch. Oh my goodness, 05:45. I bet I was popular down there on the ground. However, just now I had more important things to worry about. Apart from anything else, my eyes wouldn't stop streaming. It must've been a reaction to the sudden awakening.

Upon my return I discovered that I went from fast asleep to airborne in a Lightning supersonic fighter in just 3 minutes 45 seconds!

Climbing to 10,000 feet I contacted Crabtree. They vectored me towards an "unknown", at least they vectored me towards the last position that they saw the unidentified blip because it had since faded from their screen. As I approached the area I descended to about 1,500 feet, my eyes still would not stop streaming and I had to wipe them constantly. After patrolling the area for a while I saw a small twin-engine jet taxiing on a small airfield. Crabtree asked for the registration. This could be fun! I made a low pass, about 200 feet, and must have startled the pilot somewhat as it was still just after 6:00 am on a Sunday morning. It was a Cessna Citation. I got most of the letters on the first pass but had to go down again to confirm that I had the correct details. I passed the full registration and the aircraft type and colours to Crabtree. The controller acknowledged the report and vectored me to a border patrol CAP [Combat Air Patrol] at 20,000 feet,

I flew around the large racetrack pattern as the sun rose ever higher in the sky and welcomed what was going to be a glorious summer Sunday. When I returned to Gütersloh there would just be time to refuel and service the aircraft, put it back on state and have breakfast before I was relieved.

Now the fuel was getting down to recovery levels so I pointed the aeroplane back west towards Gütersloh. There was no other traffic so I was cleared straight in for the run and break at base. I kept the power well back all the way to minimize the noise, as it was still very early on a Sunday morning, and only advanced the throttles to stabilize the speed around finals at 175 knots. I reduced power as the runway came up so that I crossed the threshold at 165 and touched down at 155. Streaming the chute, I cleared the runway at 07:00.

Back in the "shed" I spoke to the controller on the telephone. The Citation was taxiing for take-off when I found him, so he was not our "unidentified" contact. It may have been a false radar blip, it may have been a flock of birds, or even smugglers in a light aeroplane. We'd probably never know. However, the air defence alert system had been exercised again and all had worked as advertised.'

XN771 first flew on 29 August 1962 and in 1968 re-entered service as an F.2A. It became 'P' in 19 Squadron on 21 March 1968, serving as such until January 1977 when it joined 92 Squadron as 'S'. (*Tony Paxton*)

F.2A XN724/F of 19 Squadron passing near the Eder Dam in 1975. Built as an F.2, XN724 first flew on 11 September 1961 and did not see squadron service until after conversion to F.2A, being issued to 19 Squadron on 18 May 1968. It was withdrawn from use on 7 December 1976 and it became a decoy at Laarbruch. (*Tony Paxton*)

Right: Lightnings of RAF Germany airborne from Decimomanau, Sardinia, during the Armament Practice Camp (APC) on the island in November 1975, beautifully photographed by Geoff Syrett from a Canberra of 85 Squadron. (*Geoff Syrett*)

Below: F.6 XS928/K of 5 Squadron in 1977. This aircraft first flew on 28 February 1967 and was issued to 11 Squadron that April. It went overseas with 74 'Tiger' Squadron in 1970 and had to be airlifted to BAe Warton by a Short Belfast for repair after suffering damage caused by a ground fire at Tengah when fuel vented onto the wing. New wings were subsequently fitted and XS928 operated later with 23 and 56 Squadrons before it joined 5 Squadron as 'K' in September 1976. By December 1977 the aircraft had been recoded 'L'. XS928 served with 5 Squadron from 1985 until it disbanded in December 1987. (*Tony Paxton*)

F.6 XR772/C of 11 Squadron with Jever-based F-104G 23+50 of the *Luftwaffe*. Although the German Air Force and the *Marineflieger* suffered a higher total loss rate of Starfighters than the RAF Lightnings, the latter's percentage losses are interpreted in some quarters as being higher than the German F-104 losses! XR772(E) was lost on 6 March 1985 when it crashed into the North Sea twenty miles north-east of Skegness. The pilot, Martin 'Tetley' Ramsey, of 5 Squadron, ejected, but he was killed when his parachute failed to deploy. The Starfighter had, eventually, the same straight-line top speeds but could never match the Lightning's rate of turn at any speed. It was not until the F-15 that the Lightning had any real competitor. (*Tony Paxton*)

Right: F.6 XR752 of 11 Squadron flown by Pete Naz, and F.3 XR718/P of 5 Squadron, flown by Paul Cooper, returning to Binbrook over the North Sea in July 1978. XR752, which was built as an F.3A, first flew on 16 June 1965. After serving in several units and squadrons, it joined 5 Squadron on 15 October 1974. On 29 September 1977 XR752, which was being flown by the CO, made a unique wheels-up landing on the Binbrook runway and travelled along it for almost 6,000 ft on its belly tank. Cat. 2 damage was repaired at a cost of £99,000 and XR752 was air-tested on 25 January 1978. It joined 11 Squadron in June 1978 but continued to be used temporarily by 5 Squadron without codes. In November 1985 the troubled XR752 suffered a fire on landing and afterwards was used as a decoy, before being scrapped in 1987. XR718 first flew on 14 December 1964 and was issued to 56 Squadron on 1 April 1965. In October 1974 it seemed that its flying days were over when it was stripped for spares and moved to the fire dump at Wattisham, but a reprieve followed, and the aircraft was rebuilt! Wattisham finally acquired the aircraft for BDR in 1987. (*Tony Paxton*)

Below: Ice station zebra. Two of 5 Squadron's Lightnings re-fuelling from a Victor over Greenland. (*Tony Paxton*)

Above: Night becomes Elektra. (*Tony Paxton*) *Below: Lightning Lightbulbs.* (*Tony Paxton*)

Pax Britannica. A superlative self-portrait. *(Tony Paxton)*

F.6 XS898/J of 5 Squadron, fitted with overwing tanks, refuelling from a basket deployed from a USAF KC-135 tanker's
boom in October 1978. On 13 February 1980 Flt Lt John
'Fynsey' Fynes of 5 Squadron, the last ever Lightning display
pilot, suffered disorientation, causing the aircraft to dive at
Mach 1.3 producing 13.5 G, which severely overstressed the
airframe, causing wing cracks, fuel leaks and undercarriage
mounting-bracket damage. Fynsey safely recovered to
Binbrook, where XS898 was declared Cat. 3, and was stripped
down and repaired with reinforcing boilerplates! Reissued to
11 Squadron on 27 March 1981, XS898 rejoined 5 Squadron in
March 1983. After service with both these squadrons and peri-
ods of storage, XS898 was bought by Mr Arnold Glass and
flown to Cranfield on 30 June 1988. (*Tony Paxton*)

Parched T-bird pulls in at the pumps, October 1978. '*During their early time on a Lightning squadron,*' recalls Tony Paxton, '*most pilots took right-seat rides to watch the more experienced hands operating the aeroplane and its weapons system. The Lightning was an easy aircraft to fly. It had to be. The task of operating the radar by day and night in all weathers was quite demanding enough without having a tricky aeroplane to fly as well. So every opportunity was taken to allow the junior guys to watch the combat-ready pilots do their stuff. Inevitably, there would be a chance to fly the aircraft from the right seat.*

Realising the problems involved, it was obvious that the in-flight refuelling probe could not be seen from the instructor's *position. However, there was a well-kept secret about tanking from the right seat. If the angle made by the windscreen centre strut and the coaming was used as a reference point and the aeroplane flown forward so that the tanker's hose passed behind the reference point, the pilot flying from the right seat could not miss making contact with the basket! Many a junior Lightning pilot has been struck with awe and admiration when, after the instructor has uttered those words with a resigned tone, "I have control", he has then made contact smoothly at the first attempt and condescendingly given control back to the hapless learner who knows that the newly revered demigod in the right seat can't even see the probe or basket!*' (*Tony Paxton*)

Above: In comes a thirsty F.6. (*Tony Paxton*)

Opposite: . . . closer and closer, easy does it! (*Tony Paxton*)

Wait for us, buddy! Two more F.6s close in on the
KC-135. (*Tony Paxton*)

Contrails from Lightnings in July 1979. (*Tony Paxton*)

Above: F.6/G of 11 Squadron in July 1979. (*Tony Paxton*)

Left: A veritable flock of Lightnings and a Victor tanker in formation on the occasion of the twenty-fifth anniversary celebrations at Binbrook, in August 1979. (*Tony Paxton*)

T.5 XS458/T of 5 Squadron over Cyprus in 1980. (This T-bird first flew on 3 December 1965 and was issued to 226 OCU in February 1966. It joined 5 Squadron on 12 January 1979 after service with the LTF). Tony Paxton recalls: '*All military fast jets are controlled by a stick in the right-hand and throttle(s) in the left; the trainer versions are generally configured in the same fashion and, indeed, the T.4 was. However, the T.5 was different. For the right-seat occupant the throttles were mounted on the right-hand side of the cramped side-by-side cockpit and the flying controls were operated by a stick with the left hand. This arrangement could cause some coordination problems during certain phases of flight, particularly formation flying and landing.*

During my course to become a weapons instructor, known in the Lightning force as an IWI, or Interceptor Weapons Instructor, but later standardized as QWI (Qualified Weapons Instructor), I remember very well my conversion to the right seat of the T5. I had coped pretty well with flying the aeroplane "back to front" but I had been concentrating very hard. The time came to return to Binbrook during my first right-seat ride in control. I was determined to fly a good approach and touchdown so I was concentrating very hard to send the correct messages to the appropriate hands. All went well during the initial phases of the instrument approach, air speed 175 knots with the aircraft stabilized on the descent in the landing con-

figuration. Approaching the runway threshold a slight reduction of power to cross the end at 165 knots; then a further reduction of power and a slight increase in back pressure on the stick to flare and touch down at 155 knots. I was delighted, an almost perfect landing. However, then I relaxed – big mistake, because I reverted to instinct.

Because of its high approach speed the Lightning used a braking parachute to shorten the landing roll. The brake chute is stowed under the lower jet pipe at the extreme rear of the fuselage; to prevent damage to the canopy the nose wheel must be firmly on the ground before the chute is deployed. Therefore the after-landing actions are to lower the nose wheel quickly onto the runway by pushing the stick forward simultaneously reducing the power by pulling the throttles rearward. Yes, you've guessed it, after my near-perfect touchdown I "lowered the nose wheel" with my right hand, and "reduced the power" with my left. The result was that we rocketed skyward because in my "relaxed" state I had, much to the amusement of my instructor in the left seat, engaged reheat and pulled the stick back! Much chastened, I flew a reasonable circuit with an acceptable touchdown and managed to carry out the correct actions to bring the aircraft safely to taxi speed. I bought a few beers that evening.' (T.5 XS458's last operational use was with 11 Squadron before being purchased by Arnold Glass in 1988). (*Tony Paxton*)

F.6 XR755/BJ of 11 Squadron in 1980. Built as an F.3A, this aircraft first flew on 15 July 1965 and was issued to 5 Squadron. In 1967 it was modified to F.6 standard and went on to enjoy long service with 5 and 11 Squadrons. It flew for the last time in December 1987 and in 1988 was bought by Castle Air in Cornwall. (*Tony Paxton*)

While 5 Squadron was deployed on its APC at Akrotiri, Cyprus, for live gunnery practice in the summer of 1984, three of its 'Barley Grey'-painted F.6s (first adopted in the summer of 1981) had shark's teeth markings added (to XR770/AA, the Boss's aircraft, XR754/AE, and XS903/AM) to their forward fuselages. XR770 was no stranger to different colour schemes; in 1966 at the SBAC Display, it was flown on ten occasions wearing Saudi Arabian markings. On 26 September this F.6 was issued to 74 Squadron, where it acquired the famous Tiger black-and-yellow scheme. 5 Squadron's shark's teeth markings were retained for several weeks after the Squadron returned to the UK. (*David Grimer*)

Q. An 11 Squadron F.6 on QRA in the eighties. The Q Shed, a self-contained unit which housed both aircrew and ground-crew in an adjacent bungalow, was built away from the airfield hangars, adjacent to the main runway, in order that the aircraft minimised taxiing time prior to take-off. 11 Squadron maintained its full operational commitment throughout early spring 1988, including its fair share of Southern QRA duties, Missile Practice Camp (MPC) at Valley, Wales, and live gunnery practice, until the end of April 1988. (*Malcolm English*)

Right up the pipe! (*Malcolm English*)

Below: F.6s XR769/AM and XR724/AE and two F.3 Tornados of 5 Squadron, over the North Sea in December 1987. XR724/AE first flew on 10 February 1965 as an F.3. After the Squadron disbanded at Binbrook in December 1987, XR724 was fitted with over-wing tanks and used for BAe Tornado F.3 radar trials. (*Tony Paxton*)

Siamese twins. 5 Squadron's F.6 XR769/AM and Tornado F.3 CA in December 1987. XR769 first flew on 1 December 1965 and was first issued to 74 Squadron on 2 November 1966. After a long career, XR769 was allocated to 5 Squadron (again) on 15 September 1987 and was used until squadron disbandment, in December 1987. The aircraft was then operated unmarked by 11 Squadron until 11 April 1988, when it crashed off the Humber estuary following an engine fire. Flt Lt Dick Coleman RAAF, ejected safely. (*Tony Paxton*)

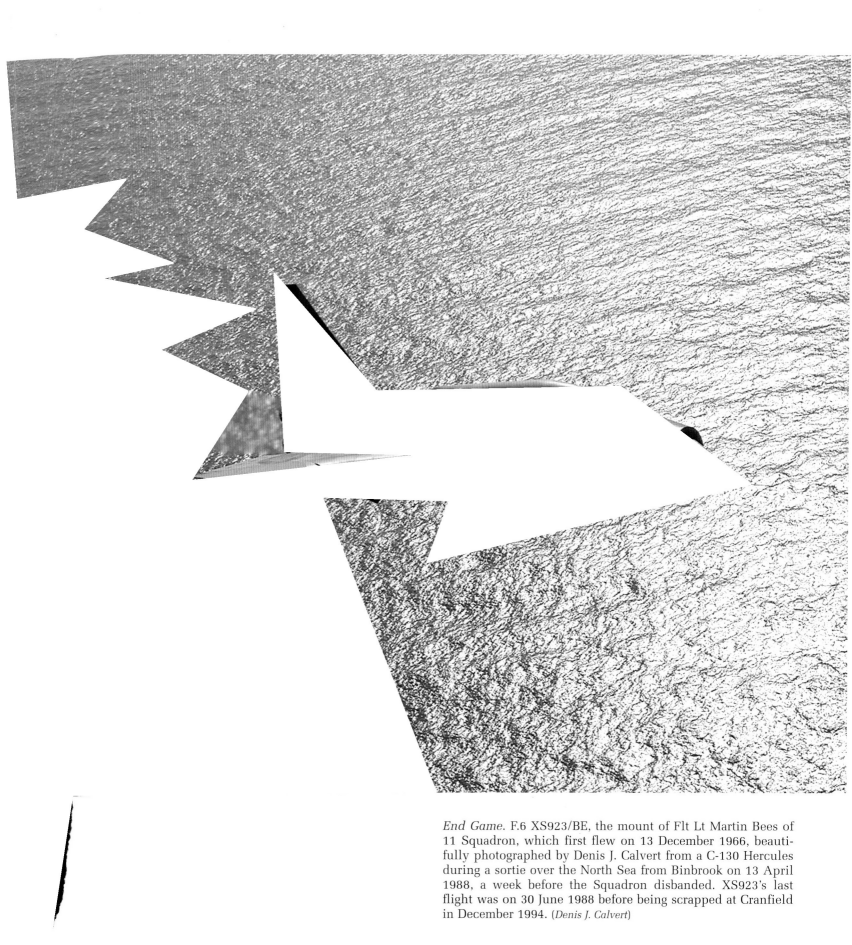

End Game. F.6 XS923/BE, the mount of Flt Lt Martin Bees of 11 Squadron, which first flew on 13 December 1966, beautifully photographed by Denis J. Calvert from a C-130 Hercules during a sortie over the North Sea from Binbrook on 13 April 1988, a week before the Squadron disbanded. XS923's last flight was on 30 June 1988 before being scrapped at Cranfield in December 1994. (*Denis J. Calvert*)

The Ultimate Lightning Museum? Bruntingthorpe airfield, Leicestershire, is now the only place in Britain where one can see a Lightning (F.6 XR728 pictured) fire up its Avons. XR728, which was built as an F.3, and first flew on 17 March 1965, made its last flight on 24 June 1988 when it was flown to Bruntingthorpe. The Lightning Preservation Group has been fortunate in acquiring the former Wattisham QRA shed to house its pair of Lightnings. The Q Shed is one of only three in the UK, the other two being at Leuchars and Binbrook. Donations are needed for funding the reconstruction at Bruntingthorpe of the Q Shed, which was donated by Trafalgar House Construction, who also paid for its dismantling at Wattisham. (*Hugh Trevor*)